BEST OF THE SUPER BOWL

THRILLING SUPER BOWL GAMES

BY DAVID J. CLARKE

SportsZone
An Imprint of Abdo Publishing
abdobooks.com

abdobooks.com

Published by Abdo Publishing, a division of ABDO, PO Box 398166, Minneapolis, Minnesota 55439.

Printed in the United States of America, North Mankato, Minnesota.
102024
012025

THIS BOOK CONTAINS RECYCLED MATERIALS

Cover Photos: Chris McGrath/Getty Images Sport/Getty Images (left); Steph Chambers/Getty Images Sport/Getty Images (middle); Rob Tringali/SportsChrome/Getty Images (right)
Interior Photos: Focus On Sport/Getty Images Sport/Getty Images, 4, 23, 24, 33; Rusty Kennedy/AP Images, 7; Brian Bahr/Getty Images Sport/Getty Images, 9; Tom DiPace/AP Images, 10; Al Pereira/Getty Images Sport/Getty Images, 13; Focus On Sport/Getty Images, 14, 34; Vernon Biever/AP Images, 16; Kevin Reece/Getty Images Sport/Getty Images, 18; Dilip Vishwanat/Sporting News Archive/Getty Images, 20; Rob Carr/Getty Images Sport/Getty Images, 21; Ross Lewis/Getty Images Sport/Getty Images, 27; Al Bello/Getty Images Sport/Getty Images, 29; Streeter Lecka/Getty Images Sport/Getty Images, 30; Allen Dean Steele/Getty Images Sport/Getty Images, 37; Al Messerschmidt/AP images, 39; Icon Sportswire/Getty Images, 41; Drew Hallowell/Getty Images Sport/Getty Images, 42; Timothy A. Clary/AFP/Getty Images, 44; Gregory Shamus/Getty Images Sport/Getty Images, 45

Editor: Charlie Beattie
Series Designer: Jake Slavik

Library of Congress Control Number: 2024938342

Publisher's Cataloging-in-Publication Data

Names: Clarke, David J., author.
Title: Thrilling Super Bowl games / by David J. Clarke
Description: Minneapolis, Minnesota: ABDO Publishing, 2025 | Series: Best of the Super Bowl | Includes online resources and index.
Identifiers: ISBN 9781098295455 (lib. bdg.) | ISBN 9798384916451 (ebook)
Subjects: LCSH: Super Bowl--Records--Juvenile literature. | American football--Juvenile literature. | National Football League--Juvenile literature. | Super Bowl--Records--Juvenile literature. | Football--United States--History--Juvenile literature.
Classification: DDC 796.332648--dc23

TABLE OF CONTENTS

CHAPTER ONE

FANTASTIC FINISHES

By the time Super Bowl XXIII kicked off in January 1989, the game was an established tradition. The championship of the National Football League (NFL) was the biggest day in American sports. Millions watched on television around the world, too.

However, the Super Bowl didn't have a history of exciting games at that point. Only once in the first 22 contests did the winning points come in the final minute. That had happened all the way back in Super Bowl V after the 1970 season. But that game was hardly a classic. It's mostly remembered for the 11 combined turnovers committed by the Baltimore Colts and Dallas Cowboys.

So football fans were ready for excitement when the San Francisco 49ers met the Cincinnati Bengals in 1989 at Miami's Joe Robbie Stadium. Both teams were known for their

San Francisco 49ers quarterback Joe Montana drops back to pass early in Super Bowl XXIII on January 22, 1989.

high-powered offenses. San Francisco had two-time Super Bowl winner Joe Montana at quarterback. Cincinnati was led by that season's Most Valuable Player (MVP), quarterback Boomer Esiason. But the game turned into a defensive struggle. The score was just 3–3 at halftime. The Bengals finally delivered a scoring boost when running back Stanford Jennings took a kickoff 93 yards for a touchdown in the third quarter.

The 49ers didn't find the end zone until the fourth. Montana hit star receiver Jerry Rice on a 14-yard touchdown pass with 14:03 left. The play tied the game 13–13. However, with just under four minutes to play, Cincinnati's Jim Breech booted another field goal. The game had been exciting. But with a combined five field goals and only two touchdowns, it wasn't yet memorable. Then the Bengals kicked off to San Francisco.

A penalty on the kickoff pushed San Francisco back to its own 8-yard line. Montana quickly got to work. With a cool confidence, he began moving the team down the field. Most of the big yards were picked up by Rice, who was in the midst of a record-setting day. With just over a minute left, he caught a pass and raced 27 yards to the Bengals' 18-yard line. It was Rice's 11th reception of the day.

Two plays later, San Francisco faced second-and-2 at the 10. Only 34 seconds remained on the clock. Montana dropped back to pass. Receiver John Taylor broke open over the middle. While Rice had been putting on a show, Taylor had not caught a pass all game.

Montana, *left*, celebrates with John Taylor, *center*, and center Randy Cross after Taylor's go-ahead touchdown catch in the final minute.

But Taylor hauled in Montana's spiral to put the 49ers ahead for good. The 20–16 final was the Super Bowl's first truly classic ending.

A DYNASTY BEGINS

Super Bowl XXXVI in February 2002 was seen as a matchup between a powerhouse and a big underdog. The St. Louis Rams had won the Super Bowl two years earlier. They had one of the best offenses in football history, led by stars such as quarterback Kurt Warner, receiver Isaac Bruce, and running back Marshall Faulk.

On the other side, the New England Patriots were seen as a "no-name" team. A year earlier, New England had been 5–11. Early in the 2001 season, star quarterback Drew Bledsoe had been knocked out with an injury. A skinny, little known, second-year backup named Tom Brady took his place.

Brady was still the starter when the Patriots met the Rams in New Orleans. And in the first half, New England raced out to a surprising 14–3 lead. New England head coach Bill Belichick's defense frustrated the Rams. Patriots' cornerback Ty Law made the biggest play by picking off a St. Louis pass and racing 47 yards for a touchdown in the second quarter.

It was 17–3 New England entering the fourth quarter. But the Rams' offense finally arrived. Warner scored on a 2-yard scramble with 9:33 left. Then, with 1:30 to go, he lobbed a pass to Ricky Proehl along the left sideline. The receiver juked around two defenders before racing to the end zone for a 26-yard touchdown catch. Kicker Jeff Wilkins's extra point tied the game.

New England took over on its own 17-yard line. The Patriots had no timeouts. With a young quarterback in the game, most people thought New England would kneel the ball down and take its chances in overtime. But Belichick and offensive coordinator Charlie Weis trusted Brady. The Patriots decided to go for the win.

Cornerback Ty Law scored New England's first points of Super Bowl XXXVI on an interception return in the second quarter.

Tom Brady threw for 53 of his 145 passing yards on the Patriots' game-winning drive in Super Bowl XXXVI.

Brady responded by showing the calmness that would help him eventually become an NFL legend. His first three passes went to running back J. R. Redmond. They totaled 24 yards. New England then faced second-and-10 from its own 41 with 29 seconds left. Brady whipped a pass over the middle to receiver Troy Brown for a 23-yard pickup. After another short completion to the 31, Brady spiked the ball to stop the clock. Only eight seconds remained.

The Patriots sent sixth-year kicker Adam Vinatieri out to try and win the game. Vinatieri had earlier made a 37-yard attempt. This time, he stepped up and blasted the ball through from 48 yards. The final was 20–17.

New England's upset win launched one of the great Super Bowl dynasties. By the time Brady left the team in 2020, the Patriots had won five more. It all started with an aggressive decision in Super Bowl XXXVI.

THE COMEBACK

The Patriots built their 2000s dynasty by seemingly always winning close games. By the 2016 season, New England had won four Super Bowls. Three of them were by three-point margins. The other had been a four-point game.

No one was predicting another close game at halftime of Super Bowl LI after the 2016 season. Facing the high-scoring Atlanta Falcons, the Patriots looked lost. Falcons quarterback Matt Ryan had thrown two touchdown passes. Brady's most memorable pass was intercepted by the Falcons' Robert Alford. The cornerback sprinted 82 yards for a touchdown to make it 21–0 Atlanta. The Patriots finally got on the board with two seconds left in the first half on a Stephen Gostkowski field goal. But they went into the break trailing 21–3. In the history of the Super Bowl, no team had ever come back from more than 10 points.

Then, with 8:31 left in the third quarter, another Ryan touchdown pass made it 28–3. The Patriots looked toast. Nobody told that to Tom Brady, though. Slowly, the Patriots started clawing back. With 2:12 left in the third, Brady hit running back James White on a five-yard touchdown pass. After Gostkowski missed the extra point, it was 28–9. The Patriots quickly got the ball back and added a field goal early in the fourth quarter.

ANOTHER OVERTIME

Super Bowl LVIII after the 2023 season featured another comeback to force overtime. The Kansas City Chiefs rallied from 10 points down to force the extra session against the San Francisco 49ers. Under the NFL's new overtime rules, both teams got a chance to score. The 49ers settled for a field goal on their first drive. Kansas City then drove down the field. A one-yard touchdown pass from quarterback Patrick Mahomes to wide receiver Mecole Hardman won the game 25–22.

Then, with 8:31 left, New England linebacker Dont'a Hightower forced a Ryan fumble. Brady took the field and quickly led a five-play, 25-yard scoring drive. A two-point conversion made it 28–20.

When the New England defense stood tall again, New England got the ball back with 3:30 left. That set the stage for one of the most amazing catches in the history of the Super Bowl. On the sixth play of the drive, Brady looked down the middle for receiver Julian Edelman. Alford tipped the ball. As it fell to the turf, four players dove to catch it. Edelman grabbed the ball, bobbled it inches from the ground, then managed to hold on with his fingertips. Four plays later, White scored again. Brady then whipped a pass to Danny Amendola. The receiver just

Julian Edelman (in white) dives to make a spectacular catch on the Patriots' game-tying drive in Super Bowl LI after the 2016 season.

snuck over the goal line to complete a two-point conversion to tie the game and force overtime.

At the time, NFL rules stated that overtime ended when the first team scored. So when New England won the toss, onlookers knew the tired Falcons defense was in trouble. Sure enough, Brady marched the Patriots down the field in less than four minutes. The ninth play of the drive was second-and-goal from the Atlanta 2-yard line. White had already caught a touchdown pass and rushed for another. This time, he took the handoff running right. Falcons corner Ricardo Allen squared White up at the line of scrimmage. But the determined running back forced his way over the goal line. What was by far the greatest comeback in Super Bowl history was complete. And the Patriots' dynasty celebrated perhaps its finest hour.

63
75

CHAPTER TWO

DEFENSIVE STANDS

Super Bowl X in January 1976 featured two of the fiercest defenses ever to take the field. The Dallas Cowboys' "Doomsday Defense" had led the team to three Super Bowls. The Pittsburgh Steelers' "Steel Curtain" helped the team become an NFL powerhouse. Not surprisingly, Super Bowl X became a slugfest.

Pittsburgh quarterback Terry Bradshaw completed only nine passes, though two of them went for touchdowns. However, his final pass came at a heavy cost. Bradshaw unleashed a 64-yard touchdown bomb to receiver Lynn Swann with 3:31 left. But just after releasing the ball, Bradshaw took a helmet-to-helmet hit from Dallas lineman Larry Cole. The score put the Steelers up 21–10. But their quarterback was done for the game.

The Dallas Cowboys "Doomsday Defense" made life tough for the Pittsburgh Steelers in Super Bowl X after the 1975 season.

Cowboys quarterback Roger Staubach (12) nearly led the team to a miracle last-second victory in Super Bowl X.

Dallas quarterback Roger Staubach hadn't fared much better. He was sacked seven times. When the Cowboys took over after Bradshaw's heroic pass, Staubach had already thrown two interceptions. But he led the Cowboys down the field and hit receiver Percy Howard on a 34-yard touchdown pass with 1:48 to go to make it 21–17. Amazingly, it was the only reception of Howard's career.

Dallas attempted to get the ball back with an onside kick. Instead, Pittsburgh recovered it at the Cowboys' 42-yard line. But the Steelers still had to get one first down to seal the game. With backup quarterback Terry Hanratty in for Bradshaw, Dallas loaded up to stop the run. The Cowboys held the Steelers on four plays. That gave Dallas the ball back with more than one minute still left to win it.

Staubach's nickname was "Captain Comeback." He quickly completed two passes to move the ball to the Steelers' 38. However, he fumbled the next snap. By the time he picked it up, Staubach had to scramble just to get an incomplete pass away. Another long attempt aimed at Howard in the end zone was broken up.

That set up one last play with three seconds left. Staubach heaved a pass toward the end zone again. Pittsburgh strong safety Mike Wagner tipped the ball at the goal line. It landed in the hands of free safety Glen Edwards. Edwards raced 35 yards back upfield. The game was over. By the time he was tackled, the Steelers were on the field celebrating their second straight Super Bowl title.

ONE MORE YARD

Entering Super Bowl XXXIV in January 2000, the St. Louis Rams' offense was the talk of the football world. It was for good reason. Quarterback Kurt Warner had come out of nowhere before the season to be named league MVP. Coach Dick Vermeil's team had rolled 526 points. Many of them came on big plays. Fans called the

St. Louis Rams quarterback Kurt Warner threw for 414 yards and two touchdowns in Super Bowl XXXIV after the 1999 season.

offense the "Greatest Show on Turf." The Rams finished 13–3 and rolled into the Super Bowl against the Tennessee Titans.

The Rams' defense had also been one of the best in the league that year. And the Rams shined on that side of the ball in a Super Bowl that turned into a low-scoring contest. St. Louis slowly built a 16–0 lead as the defense shut down the Titans' star duo of quarterback Steve McNair and running back Eddie George.

Late in the third quarter, the Titans started to climb back. George scored on two short touchdown runs, but the Titans failed on a two-point conversion after the first. Kicker Al Del Greco evened the score at 16–16 with just over two minutes left.

The Rams got the ball back. And on the first play of the drive, the offense finally got its big play. Warner launched a 73-yard touchdown pass to receiver Isaac Bruce to put the Rams ahead with 1:54 to go. Now it was up to McNair to create a miracle.

McNair was known as a clutch quarterback. He used a mix of scrambles and short passes to move Tennessee down the field. Then, with 22 seconds left, McNair escaped heavy pressure and threw a 16-yard toss to receiver Kevin Dyson at the Rams' 10-yard line. The only problem was that the play had taken 16 seconds off the clock. Tennessee called timeout with a chance to take one more snap in hopes of tying the game.

The Titans called a play for Dyson to cut over the middle of the field. He caught McNair's pass in stride at the 4-yard line. As Dyson moved toward the end zone, Rams linebacker Mike Jones wrapped his arms around the receiver's waist. That stopped Dyson's forward movement. As Jones brought him to the turf, Dyson tried to stretch the ball toward the goal line. His knee hit with the ball one painful yard short of tying the game. St. Louis's historically good offensive

Kevin Dyson (87) lunges for the end zone as he is hauled down by St. Louis's Mike Jones on the last play of the game.

team had won its first Super Bowl thanks to one of the greatest defensive plays in NFL history.

BUTLER STEPS IN

Some of the Super Bowl's biggest moments have come after coaches and players have made gutsy decisions. But at the end of Super Bowl XLIX in February 2015, one head coach made what many remember as a terrible mistake. And it set the stage for one of the biggest defensive moments in the game's history.

The Seattle Seahawks entered the game as defending champions. They were facing the feared New England Patriots. But New England had not won the Super Bowl in 10 years. In that time, the team had lost the big game twice. Super Bowl XLIX was pitted as a Seattle team trying to build a dynasty against a New England club trying to get back to its championship ways.

The game lived up to the billing. Seattle built a 24–14 lead heading into the fourth quarter. But legendary Patriots quarterback Tom Brady threw two late touchdown passes to put New England ahead 28–24.

Seattle got the ball back with just under two minutes remaining. Quarterback Russell Wilson wasted no time. His first pass was a 31-yard toss to star running back Marshawn Lynch. Later in the drive, Wilson connected with receiver Jermaine Kearse on a 33-yard toss that moved the ball to the Patriots 5-yard line. On the play, Patriots cornerback Malcolm Butler tipped the ball and seemingly broke

DONALD DOMINATION

The Los Angeles Rams led the Cincinnati Bengals 23–20 as the seconds ticked down in Super Bowl LVI in February 2022. But they needed to stop Cincinnati quarterback Joe Burrow to clinch the win. With 48 seconds left, Cincinnati faced fourth-and-1 at the Rams' 49-yard line. Los Angeles's star defensive tackle Aaron Donald burst through the line to pressure Burrow. When the quarterback's pass fell incomplete, the Rams were champions for the first time since moving back to Los Angeles in 2016.

up the pass. Kearse made a juggling catch while lying on his back. If the Seahawks were able to clinch the win, it was a play that was ready to live on in football lore forever.

With the ball inside the 5-yard line, football fans assumed who was going to get the call for Seattle. Lynch was one of the best running backs in football. His powerful runs made him especially tough at the goal line. On the day, he had already gained 98 yards and rushed for a three-yard touchdown. Sure enough, he gained four yards on first-and-goal to punch the ball to the 1. With less than 30 seconds left, Seattle coach Pete Carroll had a tough decision to make. Seattle had one timeout to stop the clock. If a running play didn't work, the Seahawks would have to use it.

Instead, Carroll decided to call a pass. Receiver Ricardo Lockette broke quickly over the middle. Butler was covering him and jumped up to contest Wilson's pass. As the players collided, Butler came away with the ball.

Butler was immediately swarmed by his teammates as a Super Bowl hero. But soon the talk of the play turned to Carroll's decision. With one yard to gain, he had decided not to give the ball to Lynch. It is still seen by many as one of the biggest blunders in Super Bowl history.

Malcolm Butler is mobbed by teammates after his game-sealing interception against the Seahawks.

CHAPTER THREE

SUPER THRILLERS

Many games are remembered for their thrilling finishes. But others are high-wire acts from start to finish. The Pittsburgh Steelers and Dallas Cowboys delivered an incredible 60 minutes of football in Super Bowl XIII after the 1978 season.

It was the first-ever Super Bowl rematch. The Steelers had won a tight 21–17 contest three years earlier in Super Bowl X. That game had featured a handful of memorable offensive plays. But Super Bowl XIII was an even bigger show.

Pittsburgh quarterback Terry Bradshaw got the fireworks started on the Steelers' first drive. He hit receiver John Stallworth on a 28-yard touchdown pass. Dallas quarterback Roger Staubach responded with a 39-yard toss to Tony "Thrill" Hill on the final play of the first quarter.

Dallas Cowboys running back Tony Dorsett looks for an opening early in Super Bowl XIII in January 1979.

The Cowboys' defense then got in on the act early in the second quarter. On a third-down play, Dallas's Mike Hegman ripped the ball away from Bradshaw. The linebacker raced 37 yards for a score.

Bradshaw was unfazed by his mistake. On the third play after getting the ball back, he flipped a pass to Stallworth at the Pittsburgh 35. Stallworth spun off a tackle and sprinted past three defenders to the end zone to tie the game. Later in the second quarter, Bradshaw connected with running back Rocky Bleier. The running back made a leaping grab in the end zone to put Pittsburgh up 21–14 at the half.

The second half turned on two huge Dallas errors. Late in the third quarter, Cowboys tight end Jackie Smith dropped an easy touchdown catch. Dallas had to settle for a field goal to make the score 21–17.

Midway through the fourth, Steelers running back Franco Harris raced 22 yards for a touchdown. On the next kickoff, Pittsburgh's Roy Gerela hit a low line drive. It came to Dallas lineman Randy White, who was in the game to block. White was playing with his broken right hand in a cast. He couldn't hold the ball, and his fumble was recovered by Pittsburgh linebacker Dennis "Dirt" Winston.

One play later, Bradshaw lofted an 18-yard touchdown pass to receiver Lynn Swann. Though Dallas scored two touchdowns late, it wasn't enough. Pittsburgh held on for a 35–31 win. At the time, it was the highest-scoring Super Bowl ever. And it is still remembered as one of the most exciting.

Steelers running back Franco Harris is mobbed by Pittsburgh fans after the team held off the Dallas Cowboys in Super Bowl XIII.

ON YOUR TOES

Super Bowl XLIII in February 2009 was an interesting matchup. The underdog Arizona Cardinals featured one of the league's best offenses. Quarterback Kurt Warner had three strong receivers. The best of them was the ultra-dependable Larry Fitzgerald.

However, the Cardinals were up against a stout defense. The Pittsburgh Steelers had allowed the fewest points during the 2008 season. The Steelers had also allowed the fewest passing yards.

Through three quarters, the Steelers held Arizona down. Pittsburgh built a 20–7 lead. The biggest play came from the defense. On the final play of the second quarter, Pittsburgh's star linebacker James Harrison intercepted a Warner pass at the Steelers' goal line. Harrison then chugged 100 yards for a record-setting defensive touchdown.

In the fourth quarter, the Cardinals' offense woke up. Warner hit Fitzgerald on a one-yard touchdown strike with 7:33 left. With just over three minutes to play, the Cardinals forced a safety. The score was now 20–16 Pittsburgh, and Arizona was getting the ball again. On the second play, with 2:26 left, Warner and Fitzgerald connected for a 64-yard score. Fitzgerald outraced several Steelers to the end zone to put Arizona ahead.

If the 23–20 lead held, Arizona would have pulled off the biggest comeback in Super Bowl history at the time. But the Steelers still had a chance. And they had their own clutch quarterback in

Pittsburgh's James Harrison fights his way into the end zone to complete his record-setting 100-yard interception return against the Arizona Cardinals.

Ben Roethlisberger. He quickly guided Pittsburgh's offense 72 yards to the Arizona 6 with 48 seconds left.

On first-and-goal, Roethlisberger lofted a ball for receiver Santonio Holmes in the corner of the end zone. Holmes already had eight catches, but he couldn't pull down the high pass. On the next play, Holmes ran a route to the other corner of the end zone. Roethlisberger had to get the ball over three defenders to give Holmes a chance. The receiver stretched to both bring in the pass

Santonio Holmes, *left*, caught nine passes for 131 yards and the game-winning touchdown in Super Bowl XLIII on February 1, 2009.

while keeping both of his feet on the ground. Holmes held the ball tight to his chest as teammates mobbed him. After the game, he was named Super Bowl MVP. His ninth catch put the finishing touch on a thrilling game.

RECORD BREAKERS

Many Super Bowls have been offensive shootouts. But Super Bowl LII after the 2017 season was truly unique. The offenses of the Philadelphia Eagles and New England Patriots put on a show unlike anything the NFL had ever seen.

The teams combined for nine touchdowns in the game. Six of them came on plays longer than 10 yards. When the game was over, the Patriots had rolled up a Super Bowl-record 613 yards. The Eagles had 538. The combined total of 1,151 was a record for any NFL game, regular season or playoffs.

The Eagles got off to the hotter start. A 34-yard touchdown pass and 21-yard scoring rush helped Philadelphia build a 15–3 second quarter lead. The Patriots finally scored their first touchdown with 2:04 left in the second quarter on a 26-yard rush by running back James White. But the Eagles responded with a trick play. Tight end Trey Burton tossed a one-yard score to quarterback Nick Foles, and it was 22–12 Philadelphia at the half.

Just a year earlier, New England had erased a 25-point third quarter deficit to win Super Bowl LI against the Atlanta Falcons. Tom Brady and the Patriots showed they weren't worried this time around. Brady threw three second-half touchdowns. The third was a four-yard toss to tight end

QUARTERBACK DUEL

Super Bowl LVII in February 2023 was the first to feature two Black starting quarterbacks. Jalen Hurts of the Philadelphia Eagles and Patrick Mahomes of the Kansas City Chiefs put on a show. Hurts threw for 304 yards and a score while rushing for 70 yards and three touchdowns. But Mahomes topped him by throwing three touchdown passes and engineering a last-second drive for the game-winning field goal. Kansas City won 38–35.

Rob Gronkowski with 9:22 left in the fourth quarter. It gave New England the lead for the first time, 33–32.

On the next drive, the Eagles faced fourth-and-1 at their own 45 with 5:39 left. Head coach Doug Pederson decided to go for it, and Foles connected with tight end Zach Ertz for two yards to keep the drive going. Just over three minutes later, the pair hooked up on an 11-yard touchdown pass. Though the Eagles couldn't complete the two-point conversion, they still led 38–33.

That gave the Patriots the ball back with a chance to win on a touchdown. This time, the Eagles ended the offensive showdown with two big defensive stops. First, a fumble recovery by defensive end Brandon Graham set up a 46-yard field goal with 1:10 left.

The Patriots got the ball back with a chance to tie the game. They drove to midfield. But Brady's miracle heave for the end zone was knocked down as time expired. The Eagles celebrated their first Super Bowl win after one of the NFL's most amazing games.

Philadelphia defensive lineman Brandon Graham, *right*, delivered the key defensive play in the fourth quarter of Super Bowl LII in February 2018.

CHAPTER FOUR

DEFINING MOMENTS

The Super Bowl was born when the NFL and the American Football League (AFL) decided to merge in the mid-1960s. The plan was for the AFL teams to join the NFL starting in the 1970 season. But before then, they would play an annual championship game. It was called the "AFL-NFL Championship Game" when first played on January 15, 1967. The NFL's Green Bay Packers won that championship by blowing out the Kansas City Chiefs 35–10. They cruised to victory the next year too, beating the AFL-champion Oakland Raiders 33–14.

Few football observers were surprised. The NFL had been around for more than 40 years. The AFL had been created in 1960. Most football fans took the Packers' wins as a sign that the NFL was a much better league.

After the Green Bay Packers dominated the first two Super Bowls, many football observers thought the NFL was far better than the AFL.

In January 1969, the New York Jets won the AFL. The Baltimore Colts claimed the NFL crown. The two teams met in Miami to determine the ultimate champion. It was the first time the championship was officially called the *Super Bowl*. Not that anyone expected a super game. Everyone favored the Colts to win.

All these predictions started to bug Joe Namath. The Jets' quarterback was flashy, brash, and confident. When one fan heckled him in the week before the game that the Jets were going to be crushed, Namath made a bold prediction. He told everyone who would listen that the Jets would be champions.

CHANGING THE VIEW

The idea that AFL teams were inferior to those from the NFL was proved wrong in Super Bowl III. But that was just the beginning. The Jets' win in 1969 kicked off a stretch of four Super Bowls in six seasons that were won by teams that had started in the AFL.

Namath's guarantee drew national attention. More than 41 million people tuned in on television to see if he could back it up. In a muddy game, the Jets won 16–7. The contest wasn't a thriller. Namath threw for 206 yards and zero touchdowns. Colts quarterbacks Johnny Unitas and Earl Morrall combined for only 17-of-41 passing and four interceptions. It might have faded into history as an uninspired championship game if not for Namath's words. The "guarantee" helped make the Super Bowl a must-see event. Each year throughout the 1970s, more and more fans tuned in. Today, the game is seen by more than 100 million people around the world.

WIDE RIGHT

Super Bowl XXV in January 1991 was the first modern Super Bowl in many ways. It was the first to feature a popular musical act at halftime. The boy band New Kids on the Block performed. The teams wore patches on their uniforms to celebrate the game's

Ottis Anderson of the New York Giants was the MVP of Super Bowl XXV in January 1991. He rushed for 102 yards and a touchdown.

25th anniversary. Today, Super Bowl teams wear specially designed patches every year.

The other new thing about Super Bowl XXV was that it was an exciting game. Few of the first 24 had been close. But the New York Giants and Buffalo Bills took the contest right down to the final kick.

The Bills entered the game with a high-powered offense. The Giants were known for their defense. And even though it was a low-scoring game in the first half, the Bills took the early 12–3 lead. The Giants then scored with 30 seconds left in the first half to cut the lead to 12–10.

New York got the ball to start the second half. It was part of the team's strategy to move the ball slowly. That way, the Bills' flashy offense would be stuck on the sidelines. The Giants' first drive took 9:29 off the clock. On the 14th play, running back Ottis Anderson scored a one-yard touchdown to put New York ahead 17–12.

The Bills retook the lead with a 31-yard touchdown run on the first play of the fourth quarter from star running back Thurman Thomas. New York got the ball and ran nearly seven minutes off the clock. Matt Bahr ended it with a field goal and it was 20–19 Giants.

After the teams traded punts, the Bills got the ball back on their own 19-yard line with 2:16 to play. Quarterback Jim Kelly maneuvered the offense to the Giants' 29 with eight seconds to play. Buffalo coach Marv Levy sent kicker Scott Norwood on to win the game. With the pressure on his shoulders, Norwood blasted his kick, then watched

Giants defensive back Roger Brown, *left*, celebrates after Bills kicker Scott Norwood, *right*, missed a potential game-winning field goal in the final seconds of Super Bowl XXV.

it slowly drift wide to the right. The Giants swarmed the field to celebrate. It was the first time the Super Bowl had been decided by one point.

ALMOST PERFECT

In 1972, the Miami Dolphins finished the regular season 14–0. They then won two playoff games and finished the year with a 14–7 victory over Washington in Super Bowl VII. Even before the Super Bowl era, no NFL team had finished a year perfect. And entering the 2007 season, the Dolphins were still the only perfect champions.

In 2007, the NFL season was 16 games long. And the New England Patriots raced through the regular season. Led by quarterback Tom Brady and receiver Randy Moss, the Patriots put up an NFL-record 589 points. Their defense allowed only 274.

New England then won two playoff games to reach the Super Bowl 18–0. There they faced a Giants team that had scuffled through a 10–6 record. That was good enough only for a wild card playoff spot. Even after the Giants won three tight road games to reach the Super Bowl, no one gave them a chance against New England.

However, New York turned in a memorable performance. The team's stellar defensive line was led by ends Michael Strahan and Justin Tuck. The group harassed Brady all game. The Patriots quarterback was sacked five times.

Still, New England took a 14–10 lead with 2:42 left on a six-yard touchdown pass from Brady to Moss. The Giants took the field needing a strong drive from quarterback Eli Manning to pull the upset. It looked hopeless with 1:15 left and the Giants faced

Tom Brady, *left*, threw an NFL-record 50 touchdown passes in 2007. Randy Moss, *right*, caught 23 of them to set another all-time mark.

New York receiver Plaxico Burress, *left*, hauls in the game-winning touchdown pass to seal the Giants' upset of New England in Super Bowl XLII on February 3, 2008.

third-and-5 from their own 45. Manning was swarmed by pass rushers but managed to escape. He then heaved a 32-yard pass down the middle of the field. Little-used receiver David Tyree leaped for it at the same time as Patriots star defensive back Rodney Harrison. As Harrison dragged him the turf, Tyree clung to the ball. He only secured the catch by pinning the ball to his helmet as he hit the turf. The "helmet catch" instantly became one of the defining plays in Super Bowl history. Four plays later, Manning lobbed the winning score to receiver Plaxico Burress.

The 17–14 upset shocked football. The Patriots had still won more games than the perfect 1972 Dolphins. But they had come up short in the Super Bowl. The memorable performance thwarted New England's dreams of perfection.

HONORABLE MENTIONS

SUPER BOWL V JANUARY 17, 1971

The Dallas Cowboys and Baltimore Colts fought through 59 mistake-filled minutes. The teams combined for a Super Bowl-record 11 turnovers. But the final 60 seconds gave fans the Super Bowl's first stunning finish. Baltimore kicker Jim O'Brien booted home a 32-yard field goal with five seconds left to win it 16–13.

SUPER BOWL XIV JANUARY 20, 1980

The three-time champion Pittsburgh Steelers entered the contest as heavy favorites over the 9–7 Los Angeles Rams. Instead, the Rams hung with Pittsburgh for three quarters and even led 19–17. But two fourth-quarter touchdown passes from MVP Terry Bradshaw made the difference. Pittsburgh eventually won 31–19.

SUPER BOWL XXXII JANUARY 25, 1998

The 1997 season was Denver Broncos quarterback John Elway's 15th in the NFL. The popular star had lost three Super Bowls. But his underdog Broncos outlasted the defending-champion Green Bay Packers 31–24. Elway's commitment to winning was on display on a third-quarter scramble. He took on three defenders, who spun the 37-year-old around in mid-air. The "helicopter" play set up a key touchdown from star running back Terrell Davis. Davis scored again with 1:45 left to put the Broncos up for good.

John Elway

Cooper Kupp

SUPER BOWL XXXVIII

FEBRUARY 1, 2004

Two years after winning a thriller over the St. Louis Rams, the Patriots were locked in another tight game with the Carolina Panthers. The teams combined for 37 points in the fourth quarter. Patriots kicker Adam Vinatieri booted through the game-winning field goal with four seconds left. New England won 32–29.

SUPER BOWL XLVI FEBRUARY 5, 2012

Four years after ruining New England's perfect 19–0 season in the Super Bowl, the New York Giants upset the Patriots again. This time, New York trailed 17–15 with 3:46 left to play. But quarterback Eli Manning tossed an incredible 38-yard sideline pass to Mario Manningham on the first play of a nine-play drive. Running back Ahmad Bradshaw scored to secure the 21–17 win with 57 seconds left.

SUPER BOWL LVI FEBRUARY 13, 2022

The Los Angeles Rams were trailing the Cincinnati Bengals 20–16 with 6:13 left. But quarterback Matthew Stafford led an incredible 18-play drive that included three third-down conversions and one on fourth down. Stafford capped it off by hitting game-MVP Cooper Kupp on a one-yard touchdown pass with 1:45 left.

GLOSSARY

clutch
Performing well in an important situation that often decides a competition or game.

dynasty
A team that has an extended period of success, usually winning multiple championships in the process.

heckled
Taunted or made fun of.

legend
A player who is generally regarded as one of the best to ever play.

powerhouse
A strong team or player.

sack
A tackle of the quarterback behind the line of scrimmage before he can pass the ball.

safety
A score of two points for a team when its opponent is unable to advance the ball out of its own end zone.

scramble
A run by a quarterback on a play where he initially intends to pass.

two-point conversion
An option for teams that have scored a touchdown to try a running or passing play from the 2-yard line for two points, instead of kicking for one point.

underdog
The person or team that is not expected to win.

upset
An unexpected victory by a supposedly weaker team or player.

wild card
Made the playoffs without winning the division.

MORE INFORMATION

Books

Graves, Will. *GOATs of Football*. Abdo, 2022.

Hanlon, Luke. *Football Strategies*. Abdo, 2024.

Stathes, Corbu. *Everything Football*. Abdo, 2025.

Online Resources

Booklinks
NONFICTION NETWORK
FREE! ONLINE NONFICTION RESOURCES

To learn more about the Super Bowl's most thrilling games, please visit **abdobooklinks.com** or scan this QR code. These links are routinely monitored and updated to provide the most current information available.

INDEX

About the Author

David J. Clarke is a freelance sportswriter. Originally from Helena, Montana, he now lives in Savannah, Georgia.